The Standard Publishing Company, Cincinnati, Ohio.
A division of Standex International Corporation.
© 1992 by The Standard Publishing Company
All rights reserved.
Printed in the United States of America.
99 98 97 96 95 94 93 92   5 4 3 2 1

Library of Congress Cataloging-in-Publication Data
Watson, Elaine.
All about hands / Elaine Watson ; illustrated by Roberta K. Loman.
ISBN 0-87403-951-7
Library of Congress Catalog Card Number 91-46613

ALL ABOUT HANDS

Elaine Watson
illustrated by Roberta K. Loman

STANDARD PUBLISHING™

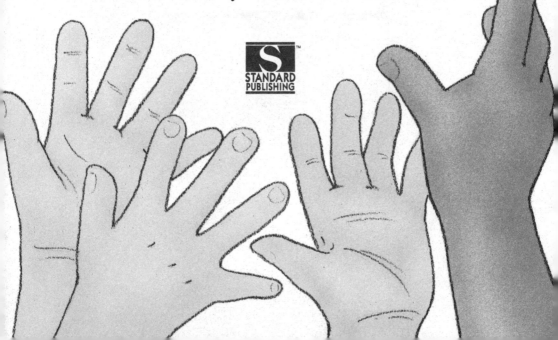

"Clap your hands, all you people."

Psalm 47:1
International
Children's Bible

God planned for hands.

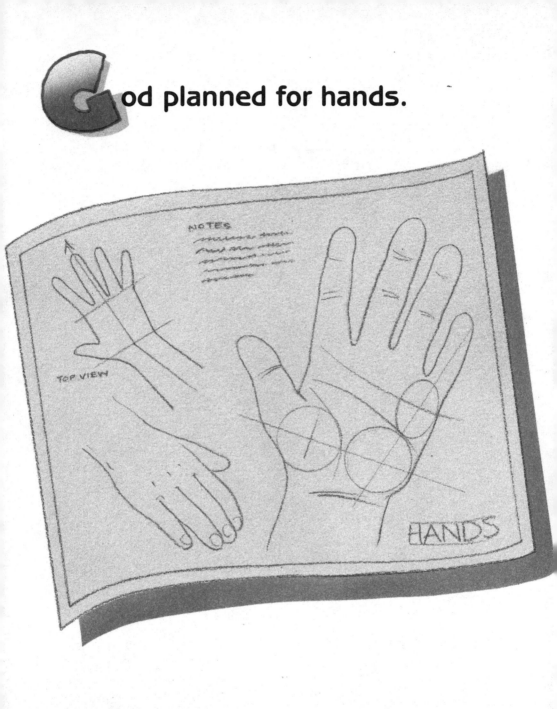

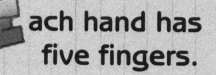

You have one hand at the end

Each hand has
five fingers.

You have
a right hand

of each arm.

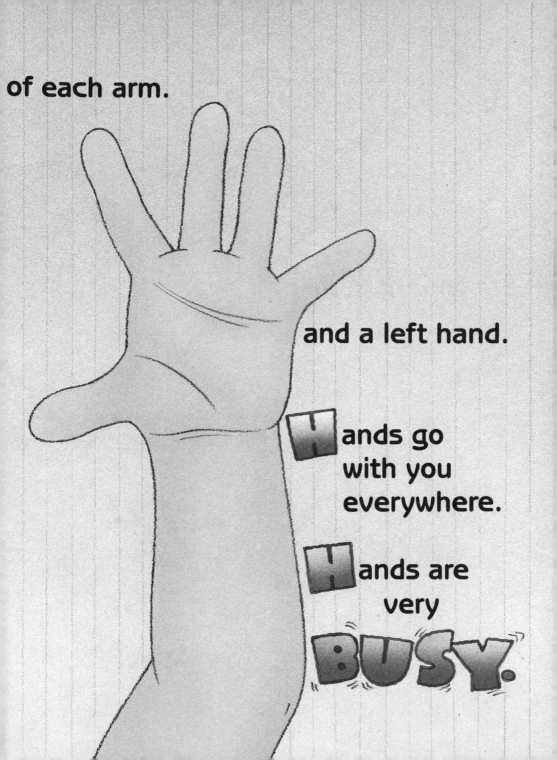

and a left hand.

Hands go
with you
everywhere.

Hands are
very

BUSY.

Hands hold things . . .

your hairbrush,

your Bible,

your spoon,

your doll.

 **ands like to HELP.**

**They help you
get dressed in the morning.**

Hands button button buttons.

They make zippers go **UP** and **DOWN** and they *try* to tie shoelaces.

ands help Daddy
paint the doghouse.

ands help Mommy
wash the dog.

Hands like to touch things . . .
soft **FUZZY**
baby chicks

and the turtle's
hard shell.

Hands work puzzles.

ands
stack blocks
TALL.

Hands pound clay
FLAT.

There are other things

Hands like to CLAP.

hands can do.

Hands like
to

WAVE.

Hands like
to give . . .

food to the birds
when snow is
on the ground

and an offering
at Sunday school.

Hands like to pray.

Thank You, God, for hands that

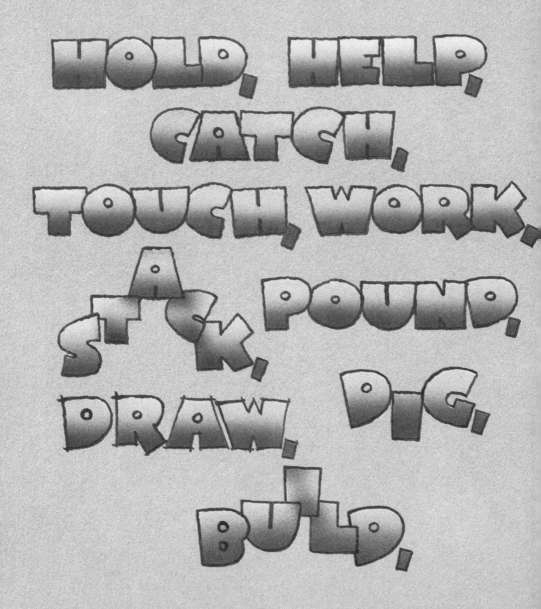

HOLD, HELP, CATCH, TOUCH, WORK, A STICK, POUND, DRAW, DIG, BUILD,

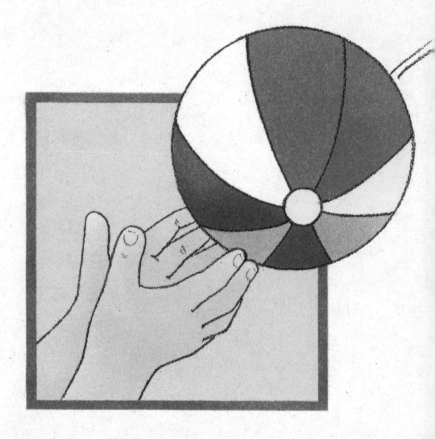